Stephen McKenna

Stephen McKenna

PERSPECTIVES OF EUROPE
1980 – 2014

curated by
Alix Collingwood and Michael Dempsey

Middlesbrough Institute of Modern Art

Dublin City Gallery The Hugh Lane

2015

ARTIST'S ACKNOWLEDGEMENTS

I am extremely grateful to the many people who have helped and collaborated in the production of this catalogue and the organisation of the associated exhibitions.

The first proposal came from Gavin Delahunty and Kate Brindley, previously Curator of Exhibitions and Director at mima. Their initiative has been admirably brought to fruition by Alix Collingwood. The invitation to extend the exhibition to the Hugh Lane came from its Director, Barbara Dawson, and the curatorial work has been led by Michael Dempsey.

The suggestion of the theme 'Europe' for an exhibition was made by Linda Morris, who has been familiar with my work for many years. In his outstanding essay, David Fraser Jenkins, a long time friend and supporter, has greatly expanded this idea and placed my itinerant career in an art historical context. The Kerlin Gallery and their staff have been of the greatest help in tracing paintings and making them available for viewing.

The preparatory work on the catalogue would have been impossible without the dedicated assistance of BethAnn Roch and Susan McKenna Fialho.

I am particularly grateful to the private and public collectors who have so generously agreed to loan works to the two exhibitions.

TABLE OF CONTENTS

Middlesbrough Institute of Modern Art

PREFACE
Alix Collingwood, Curator, Middlesbrough Institute of Modern Art

Stephen McKenna is a distinguished and precise artist, accomplished and internationally renowned. Throughout his long career, spanning six decades, he has lived and worked in various countries, but since 1998 he has been based in Ireland, in an old schoolhouse in Bagenalstown, County Carlow. And it was here that the exhibition accompanying this publication between mima, Middlesbrough and the Hugh Lane, Dublin began to come to fruition. Surrounded by dozens of paintings and canvases it becomes obvious just how central the concepts of travel and landscape are to McKenna and it was around these elements that we chose the theme of the exhibition. It is the artist's response to a lifetime spent travelling and living in countries the length and breadth of Europe.

The exhibited paintings and drawings, made between 1980 and the present, reflect not only the cities, the landscapes, the people and the artefacts of the various countries, but also their history and the contents of their museums. In his paintings McKenna is able to show such intensity that standing in front of them, immersed, you are almost certainly there, in that place, sensing the landscape.

For mima McKenna has curated a selection of his drawings to accompany the paintings. Drawing is one of the most fundamental forms of artistic expression, it is immediate in its honesty. For McKenna drawing is an inherent part of his practice – a way to order his responses and senses, a diary. Although these may begin as sketches for much larger paintings, within the context of this exhibition they represent another side to the artist's practice. They are his immediate response to a view, an experience.

Drawing as an artistic practice is of unique resonance for Middlesbrough; mima was built, in part, upon the legacy of The Cleveland International Drawing Biennial 1973 to 1996. Through the Biennial, drawing has now become intimately associated with mima and embedded in almost all of what we do; its ability to discover, articulate and challenge our understanding of its very principles are reflected throughout our programmes.

In our selection of drawings for this exhibition we have been careful to introduce new subject matter not seen in the paintings, presenting a unique insight into this less familiar part of McKenna's practice.

This book would not have been possible without the support and enthusiasm of Barbara Dawson and Michael Dempsey at the Hugh Lane, Dublin, David Fraser Jenkins, the Kerlin Gallery and all those who have so kindly loaned work, both museums and private collectors. We are, of course, indebted to Stephen McKenna for his immense passion and tireless dedication to the project and are extremely privileged not only to bring this exhibition, the artist's largest for ten years, to Middlesbrough, but to be the opening venue for this outstanding collection.

PREFACE

Barbara Dawson, Director, Dublin City Gallery The Hugh Lane

This exhibition, 'Perspectives of Europe' – paintings by Stephen McKenna, reveals the artist's enduring pursuit of the 'Classical' restraint in the painted image. His is a keen and original vision which is informed by his practice and the millennia of Western mythology and its history. Although he draws upon the poetry of the past Mckenna does not consider his work as part of a continuum. However it is part of the canon that will make up the future history of European painting. London born with strong associations with Donegal, McKenna studied at the Slade School of Art, but left London in pursuit of his artistic career, eschewing the predominant trends of abstraction and conceptual art. His travels in Europe, including living in Germany and Italy. saw him seek out resolutions in European classicism in art and architecture, paintings by old masters and the structures of the great European cities – urban, rational, ordered. Although he could be considered part of the London School of Art, this sense of displacement makes Stephen McKenna stand outside that tradition. McKenna's cities are analytical compositions observing the human scale in the built environment and the natural rhythm of their architectures. His very particular vision is rich in allegory and bathed in tangible light giving us new experiences of often familiar terrain. And it is the experience of the painting itself that McKenna leaves for us to encounter.

McKenna's interest in science leads to his appreciation of the rational structure of the natural world, and appreciation of formal landscape according to the artist – "grows out of this enjoyment of man's ability to mould the natural condition, to ape the creative power of God". Alongside his paintings of cities, in this exhibition there is a focus on the artist's paintings of trees. McKenna's trees are a particular species. He delights in opening his eyes and our eyes to the poetry contained in their painterly representation – ordinary and extraordinary in their compositional structures. Swathed in precise and detailed foliage they make one aware of the workings of the classical spirit in its environment and it is this exposure that makes his work unique.

We are privileged to present 'Perspectives of Europe', Stephen McKenna's first exhibition in the Hugh Lane in collaboration with mima, Middlesbrough Institute of Modern Art. In selecting this exhibition we had both a great pleasure and quite a challenge given the extraordinary and prodigious output of this celebrated painter. Our thanks to all of our lenders without whose support this exhibition could not have happened; to Alix Collingwood Curator mima; Michael Dempsey Head of Exhibitions and Logan Sisley Exhibitions Curator and all of the Gallery's staff.

Dublin City Gallery The Hugh Lane

RATHMULLAN TOPE 8527/D 57 × 80 cm 1985 pencil Cat.118

Germania and Italia

THE RATHMULLAN TOPE

This drawing of a fish, obviously recently caught and now lying on some slab, makes it look massive on its good-sized sheet of paper more than thirty inches across. The paper has been delicately touched with a few outlines, but is mostly shaded and textured repeatedly with dancing gentle strokes of pencil, hovering over the rounded surface, nowhere heavy, so that it is only the long rhythm of the body and the absence of anything superfluous, apart from the torpedo fins and flukes, that give such a feeling of weight to the body. The signature initials beside its tail are so dwarfed that they look like one of the small Hollanders gawping at the beached whale in Goltzius's famous print. This drawing has a feeling of an immense scale, a rare and wonderful quality that is achieved only by simplification of detail within a convincing and lifelike apprehension, helped along here by the way that the fish is so long that it seems to push against either edge of the paper. The 'tope' is a kind of shark, found all around Britain but was here at Rathmullan in Donegal. At that time in 1985 it was the victim of an annual sport, one of many caught on a line and brought ashore for the fun and brag of it, since this fish cannot be eaten. Nowadays they would all be returned to the sea, but then they were simply left in a heap on the quayside, for McKenna to heave one home in the boot of his car, and get about two days to draw and paint before it decayed.

All this is very well, but there is something more. This beautiful, dead and squandered animal, with its blank eye, has been so visually caressed, its changes of shape and surface recorded and summarised as a record of the prolonged staring by the artist, that its death has become a felt loss, and its appearance a homage to the self-contained and passionless natural world. It was murdered for no purpose, and while it still for a short time looks powerful its presence has taken on the quality of a sacrifice, as if we were watching with horror the carcass of a bull being towed insultingly by a tractor out of a Spanish or Provencal ring. This is what art can do, conjure such an emotional force, through observation and feeling that is re-presented. The really quite ordinary thing that we are shown comes to imply, and wholly without words, a mute moral presence.

McKenna is of course aware of this double reading of an image as both description and emotion, and he has re-told in an essay the classic statement by Panofsky of the different levels of understanding of art (1997, p.14). But he revised these principles, firstly to point out that still life painting and abstraction, which Panofsky thought more or less hum-drum, did indeed carry secondary meanings, since they were made within the many existing conventions of these arts, and picked up references from predecessors. And more importantly, McKenna laid out the ways in which the primary subject of representation is not straightforward, but in itself "is informed by the mind and spirit, with all their memories and ideals". The art of painting, of transferring visual experience into colours on a flat surface, requires a degree of mental commitment, with all kinds of implications. And much earlier, in an interview, he had stated directly of still life painting "However simple the form and structure of the objects chosen, that does not prevent them having symbolic or allegorical properties" (1981).

Art shows, but it cannot tell, and it puts the responsibility onto us. The poor tope grants us its appearance as a sacrifice, but who knows, the Spanish may have been correct in believing that to watch the *corrida* can expiate the power of death.

ORIGINS AND LOYALTIES

"Yes", replied McKenna, in an annoying but revealing way, when someone asked him, in a published but evidently revised conversation: "Do you consider yourself English, Irish or European?" meaning, unexpectedly, that these are not alternatives, and that he is all three (1990, p.53). He had been living in Donegal (and drawing the fish) because his father, whose family was from Tyrone, had settled there after returning to Ireland. McKenna was born just before the war in London, which he remembers when he was very young as a city in ruins and still being destroyed. The family moved to Austria in 1946, and he remembers Vienna looking as it does in the 'Third Man', with its centre under rubble and divided between three governments. At the outset of his life he was forcibly aware of this low point in modern history, which he saw from both sides. He returned to London when he was a student, and lived there for a further ten years. But only a few paintings and drawings in this exhibition are of England. Almost all are nevertheless of real places, spread around Italy, Ireland, Germany, Portugal and the Mediterranean.

It is difficult to think of another painter – apart from the topographers – who has been committed to so many places around Europe. McKenna was for a time a wanderer, living in Belgium, Germany, Italy and Ireland, and travelling across the whole Continent from these centres to stay for short periods of study elsewhere, and while on his way learning to speak French, German and Italian. He had made the decisive move to Germany from London in 1971, so abandoning an English stance, and furnishing himself with a total change in geographical outlook, becoming an insider on the mainland of Europe, able easily to drive to any country as if a part of his own world (while still sometimes returning to a base in London).

It seems that living in Germany brought into the foreground for McKenna an historic northerly topic in the fine arts, the problematic attraction between 'Germania and Italia', which amounts to an admiration and envy of Mediterranean culture when it was touchably close, yet so different. He was able in 1981 to re-animate in a new version Poussin's painting of the blind Orion, now presenting this giant as an artist, wandering, in search of new eyesight and new love, guided by an Intelligence but heading towards, in this version, an ancient and specifically German city. McKenna was earning his living, of course, from his art, teaching, selling paintings and seeking commissions, building in each place a reciprocal relation with the country.

Like some grand old Renaissance scholar in the manner of Erasmus, who could move from place to place and talk to equals within the lingua franca of the classics, McKenna made visual homecomings with the picture galleries of Europe, feeling his way into what he called "the art of painting as it is, and always was" (1997 p.12), and deepening his ambition to revive this art from its fundamentals. The course of his art since the 1970s provides a network of associations with what was becoming a particular taste for old and modern masters of European painting. To start with, there were overt quotations – a figure from Titian, several from Stubbs, an idea from Dosso Dossi – but gradually as he studied the nineteenth and early twentieth century painters face to face, the references he made became embedded, not strident, internalised into a transforming sense of air, enabled by considerable technical, but hidden, expertise. It was a move from a learned and still academic practice to one that was instinctive, and this is clear in the course of this exhibition. This project was advanced also through his study of art history, and his beginning to amass what has become a library of the key artists, and writing lectures and essays on questions of principle. He was also studying systematically the technique of painting, though for direct guidance at the time there was only Ralph Mayer's 'The Artist's Handbook' in the edition of 1951.

The paintings and drawings exhibited here were made over the last thirty-five years, the second half of McKenna's career, while he was living mostly in Italy and then Ireland, and incessantly travelling to sites he wanted to paint. A few of the pictures, the oldest ones here, are overtly political. It may not have seemed apparent at the time, but the implicit subjects of these pictures at large are so committed and enriched that they have become a witness, and the artist a real *peintre témoins de son temps*. This becomes evident in the sheer peculiarity of his images, and in the degree to which the simpler they seem, the more they are loaded. But this will be a long process of revelation, as future eyes will look to see what they can be told.

THIS EXHIBITION

The selection for both of the slightly different exhibitions at the Middlesbrough Institute of Modern Art and at the Dublin City Gallery The Hugh Lane, has been made by the artist with the curators. Some of the paintings belong to him and others are borrowed back from the museums and people who bought them, and the drawings are all his own. He has always retained some drawings as important to him, and as a group they show the broad range of what he has done, and what it means. They are not shown in Dublin, but there was in 2014 a display of sixty of his drawings and watercolours at the Butler Gallery, Kilkenny, 'Observations and Reflections 1974–2013', none of which is included in this selection.

Each of his exhibitions is intended to provide a context for a certain kind of understanding of the individual pictures, putting similar subjects together, and particularly avoiding a display in order of date, lest a picture be read off as if a demonstration of change. This selection of the paintings emphasises cities and architecture and landscape rather more than still life and portraits. It is not a balanced array of all the kinds of work he has made over the period, so that it is not a 'retrospective' exhibition.

The choice of work goes back to when McKenna was forty, and had just left Germany for Brussels. There is always a continuity in pictures, especially if seen in retrospect, but this break in 1980 coincides with a great divide in the practice of art. When this change of tide arrived in London in the winter of 1979–80 it could be felt, extraordinarily, as a fundamental shift in the aesthetic temperature, a feeling radiating from the Royal Academy's hurriedly arranged exhibition that winter called 'The New Spirit'. This advertised the shift from modernism and a return to figurative painting. But since the time he had left the Slade School McKenna's painting had already presaged these changes, and had been a prolonged process of mostly independent learning in drawing, colouring, painting, and in the study of the painterly masters.

This was an education that was waiting to blossom into a way of living wholly within painting. And just when public taste caught up with his decade-long wish for a new start, he found that his art broke free, while being released again from the critical interest which was now in favour of brushy Expressionism which had no relevance to him. There was a new beginning for McKenna, in a sense his Opus 1, even at that period of his middle age. While he was beginning to work on his large paintings of cities he was able to create a genuine *paysage moralisé*, and it seems that his imagination caught up with his very earliest experience of real-world calamities, the sight of Europe in 1945.

And it had been during the war that McKenna, aged five, had stayed for weeks at a time in Middlesbrough, where lived his Irish grandfather and some uncles, all employed there as naval engineers. He remembers the overnight train journeys and the intimacy with heavy industry and manufacturing. He brings now, strangely, at his return, the hand-applied chemistry of painting, beginning with images that refer to that memory of the distant war, but celebrating a much closer and more equal view of Europe.

DRAWINGS

Looked at together, the drawings seem very different from each other, and were made for a variety of purposes. All his paintings apart from the still lifes are constructed from sketches on paper, usually very many, but the drawings themselves originate with an informed sight. The 'Study of Trees' (p.131) is just that, and so is 'Donegal Sea' (p.127), except that these drawings of thirty years ago were preceded and crowded by many others, some in sketchbooks, of the same places which he knew well. They are both quite old-masterly, with memories of Van Dyck and Constable and Dutch artists, without which they could not have achieved such rhythm. And they are quite different from each other, as McKenna does not possess an easy facility for seizing an image in pencil, and has to imagine each drawing as its own one-off construction.

This is not just the case of finding places that appeal, and he does not look for historic sites. The interior of 'Santa Ana Las Palmas' (p.112) is such a site, but it has an individual, orthogonal spaciousness and an empty clarity, its geometry inspiring a wish to be able to feel the space behind its central column that masks the far corner. And this is to say that it makes its point as a homage to the painting of Pieter Saenredam, at the limit Saenredam found of perspectival imperiousness. Maybe he wanted to see how Saenredam did it, or maybe the place itself suggested the comparison. It is anyway difficult to inscribe all that architecture both visually and mathematically, but the beauty of the drawing lies in the extraordinary triangle of foreground space, where the viewer's eyes suddenly splay out to left and right along the tumbling pavings.

In general the change in the drawings has been from a sunlit and shadowy chiaroscuro, as in his view of 'San Nicola in Carcere' (p.113) in Rome, to the more foggy and less forceful coloured spaces of the watercolour of 'Berlin Bode Museum' (p.115), a change which applies as much to southern buildings like 'The Bishop's Palace Porto' (p.117). But drawing is always a challenge, and looking for an unimposing life McKenna has recently been studying animals in London zoo, standing beside the cages with a pencil and pad in hand. And he has become a specialist in the habits of birds, seen just as they might be, without any of the triggers for naming them. This is birds as they feed, fly together, how they look in old Italy in Pitigliano, and in Ireland (p.122-123). Dark against the sky, birds resemble pencil marks on paper, but to fix them still within a rectangle is a trick. As with his drawings and watercolours of waves (p.126), it is a matter of finding a subterfuge that can link a graphic touch with memory, and in both cases he finds a new form for movement.

There are fewer drawings of still life because McKenna paints them directly onto the canvas, and the drawing stage is usually pre-empted by the careful choice and arrangement of the objects, an activity which itself takes on some of the actions of drawing – not making marks, but searching for shadows and the spaces between objects, and their overall balance within the frame. But sometimes he paints still life in watercolour, maybe encouraged by the watercolours of his friend Michael Williams. 'Receptacles' (p.138) is a *tour de force* of contrasting materials, including a glass water jug. McKenna has written about the way in which weaving a basket, effectively shaping a hollow space out of a long osier, and which is made only of these lines, is an echo of the painter's task (1996 p. 18). To be able to depict a transparent glass carafe in front of a basket, with another basket around it, is an outstanding performance, held in check by the apparent modesty of the objects themselves, and the comedy of their polyglot conversation. The painted background space is made to look especially artificial as it sits within the blank of the paper, and is of much the same colour as the metal pail, the colour appearing again in the carafe and the block at the left. And there is some water in the bottom of the carafe.

The sight of his 'Receptacles' twitches successive muscles at the thought of their weight, it might leave a chill at the reminiscence of Urne Buriall, and nudge a little shame at their folkish complaint against the branded shopping bag. But they are just some handy containers, collected in the way people sometimes amass favourite old hats, or nostalgic watering cans. They stand here more Caravaggio than Cézanne, not to do with visual perception but with the nature of their existence, which stops short of a complete revelation, leaving detail below a certain level that is still contained within the medium. McKenna has painted baskets often, at least since 1980, and they have become an emblem of his art.

Several grand drawings of the early 1980s gather an accumulation of details from the old masters, always put together on a small scale within the design, as if some new system of lettering, searching for an overall sentence of subject, verb and object. He had then left Germany for Brussels, and not yet moved to Italy, and they seem now an intermezzo between North and South, pitched at this level of Germania-Italia. They are usually arranged around a system of perspective that plunges the intricate staging further and further into the distance, hopping across thresholds between levels of real and pictorial. 'The Age of Reason' (p.132) is surely ironic, pitching a certain smug urbanity against a Sexual Paradise before the Fall that outdoes Cranach and Poussin in unlikely bliss, except that Hogarth's pug sits there in Protestant disapproval. And then all of the groupies are held prisoner by the blank faces of new office buildings. The proffered wine glass at the left appears to promise an impossible mix of everyday pleasure and drudgy work. But the drawing combines social life with old master freedoms and a modern lack of soul, all in separate compartments, and however much the imagination focuses on the central section with delight, the contemporary parts are disturbing. Maybe it had once had some programme, or personal reference, but these are overtaken, and to look is to seek an interpretation.

The 'Study for Clio Observing the Fifth Style' (p.134) of a few years later posits a way to deal with such a pictorial mix. It is about a way forward for painting, and is itself the beginning of that way. The Muse of History is about to write, and points to women's heads, as if images of the archaeologists' four 'styles' of Pompeian art (the large painting McKenna made from this is slightly different). Just suppose, the artist asks, that Pompeii had not been destroyed by Vesuvius, and that we could go back to that moment, and invent our own 'Fifth Style', after the life of Christ but ignoring everything since, taking it not too seriously, and matching an artist's naked model with a dancing lay figure that has sprung out of a box. The drawing is all sketchy, set on a single well-organised stage, with frames and friezes around. But art history had not stopped, and it also matches Titian (his most classical painting) and Roman art. The whole design points to the blank panel held by Clio, to say that here at last history and study can be united, and the location will be this Italian landscape that is part observed and part delivered through sculpture and architecture. What comes after this, will be what is drawn by Clio. And McKenna had by then begun to study for long weeks the ancient paintings in the ruins of Pompeii, to discover how they were made, and reform his practice.

PAINTERLY CITIES

Derry from the walls, Berlin beside the lake, London at Greenwich Park, all of them seen in the first years of the 1980s, and all huge paintings, as large as a painted landscape can decently be – this group makes an extraordinary statement of observation in politically difficult times. They are also amongst the last of McKenna's paintings using very many mixed colours, and an application of glazes and scumbles, before he revised his technique. The paintings are set at borders, Derry an outpost at the border of Northern Ireland (p.58-61), Berlin still divided and showing the East across the Havel lake (p.56), and Greenwich Park (p.51), looking across the border of nature and town, and the changes from park to the historic naval college and to the skyscrapers of the City.

There is one case of additions, and in the foreground of the painting of Derry on the river Foyle there is a murdered citizen, on his back and as if contained within a nest, and on the other a mother suckling a baby. Both figures are reminiscent of Giorgione's 'Tempesta', the most fraught of all old master landscape paintings, although the mother is borrowed from the plump Irish woman near the centre of Courbet's 'Atelier'. This was ten years after Bloody Sunday, and there is a British helicopter overhead. But the limits of the allegory are unclear – the weather is poor, the Protestant cathedral at the centre is in shadow, but there is a radiant reflection from the water. The vehicle for this expression is not primarily these allegories, but the way that the representation nestles within Courbet's technique, its breadth, the largeness of the trees, the waxy application and this highlight at the centre, since Courbet's massive forms bring with them his particular pathos.

The centre of this triptych is the coat of arms of Derry, transformed into a grey cloudiness in which the skeleton (which is genuinely part of the arms) is beckoning. The oak branches are a pun on the city's Irish name. Some of the birds here re-appear in the alarming 'Bogside' drawing, set on the city walls where a hawk seizes a rabbit, in front of a tower block with sinister figures on the roof. In the painting of the Bogside, again in gloom, there is security wire, a helicopter in the air, and lights and fences along the street, and an ancient cannon pointing over the town centre. This triptych is of the utmost gloom, neither partisan nor specific, but a record of the sheer unending misery of the Troubles.

There is a rough grain to these paintings, a refusal of detail, a burying of drawing within the layering of paint that gives a naivety to the depiction, as if nothing had been designed, but grown like mould on the surface of the painted ground. It might have been this breadth of touch that attracted McKenna to make the large painting of the ruined temple at Selinunte in Sicily (p.40), itself one of the great ruins, where the marble drums of the columns have been collected at some point and heaped onto the base. It is impossible to guess the real size of the temple, which resembles one of Guston's paintings of a hand or a foot looking immense. But it is also remarkable in what it does not do, in cutting out all romanticism from a site that would have appealed to Turner.

McKenna had retained his flat in South London, and went to the parks in Dulwich, Richmond and Greenwich to make oil sketches in the open air. These led to 'An English Oak Tree' (p.84), in which the scale and isolation of the tree are augmented, although the title was only found for it after the picture was finished. Another group of oil studies of trees lead to his painting of Greenwich Park. The preparations, as always, united the challenge of past masters, here Gaspard Poussin and Constable as well as Courbet, with an unspoken symbolism, probably itself more tied to visual observation than to any deliberation. But the painting is huge, on the scale of Seurat, and the sight of it simply demands reflection on the contrast between nature and city. The weather now is better than at Derry or Berlin, almost in praise, except that in comparison to a study for the whole picture he took a higher viewpoint for the painting to show more of the tower buildings, perhaps menacing. The broad technique again keeps at a distance both Dutch naturalism and German and English romanticism, and so holds back on limiting the implications.

The pair of Berlin paintings, made in that city, are even larger and even more pessimistic in appearance. But at the time of the paintings McKenna published 'On Landscape', repeating twice that "Painting is the link between the present world and the memory of the Golden Age, and whether in times of optimistic renewal or of stoic resignation it has the duty of preserving its own ability to see that relationship clearly" (1984, p.59). Maybe these most bleak of paintings should be taken as a bottoming-out, believing that there will be inevitably a renewal (as has, it appears, happened since).

'Berlin Havelsee' (p.56) depicts three areas receding into the distance, and almost half is an unappealing beach like a stage front. The fallen tree has re-grown, even if it is still bare in what seems to be not quite winter. There is a flood-line of litter, in the preparatory drawing just scattered about, but in the painting placed more deliberately, like fragments of lettering. Some of this rubbish is a sharp blue and green, and these elements of text and colour have a potential for life. The ruined palace is the former Italian Consulate in Berlin (p.57), the northern end of the 'Axis', and the wreck of the political alliance of Germany and Italy, and of Italian magnificence north of the Alps, Germania-Italia at its lowest. The boulders are reminiscent of Selinunte, yet have no form, and are separated from what might be a colonnade. The Consulate building appears ignored rather than damaged, as if to show that nothing had been done to come to terms with this modern history. There was a need to return to base in Italy, to start again in a purer direction.

THE ETRUSCAN STYLE

In 1986 McKenna took an easel, paints and brushes into the rooms of Roman painting at Pompeii (befriending the guards in those easier times) to copy some of the murals to find out how they had been done. The results were to alter dramatically the way he painted, both in colour and design. This study was continued, surprisingly, in New York the following winter, where he was living for six months while exhibiting there, before moving to Italy. He discovered how few colours were used by these Pompeian artists, and experimented to find a new clarity of colour, and so of southern light, in his painting. And he appears to have noted for his use the decorative screens of Pompeian painting, in which each scene, often of a garden, is blithely placed beside another, perhaps of gods, as if in some suspended frame, so there are endless sequences of pictures within pictures, beginning with the pergola of the courtyard itself.

McKenna's painting of the rooms of his own house, the Villa Palombaro near Orvieto, seen as a sequence one after the other, is a marked contrast to his previous work, suddenly looking like an innocent Dutch interior, except for a startling choice of light and dark colours that create a luminous space (p.79). This is a new mood, and the emphasis on imaginative colour is noted by two rolls of cloth, in the foreground in yellow and mauve, which set the key for the colouring of the whole picture. The colours are mottled rather than modelled (except in the jug), and are so much themselves the force of the drama that the painting falls on the eye as if it were abstract. Maybe it shows the corridor to his bedroom from the studio, so joining creative and domestic spaces, and is straightforwardly about re-making a life as a whole. But such symbolism de-values the peculiar force of the painting, which is as unsettling as a Vermeer, and full of reflections, highlights and geometrical shapes.

The two Roman paintings in this exhibition stretch this complexity. Each is designed around successive thresholds between different levels of representation, which overlap. His lessons from Roman art, and a new interest in Etruscan painting, and examples from two modern masters as well, had encouraged McKenna to find a convincing method of linking different scales within a single, new image. This procedure is vital to looking at the paintings in this exhibition, for the viewer's mind repeatedly jumps between differing understandings, leveraging off against each other the ancient and the contemporary, the personal and general, without coming to rest.

'The Yellow Window' (p.75) is based on what could be seen from the balcony of his flat in Rome, where he had moved in 1989. 'Stone Map' (p.41) shows, at the top, a different angle on this same view of the ancient city centre, the Aventine and Palatine hills. The two modern artists who had become enablers were both, though not always recognised as such, master colourists, Magritte and Hopper. McKenna had always admired Magritte, and treasured the memory of visiting his widow in their house in Brussels. Magritte had somehow been able to glide his vision evenly across opaque touches of colour, to make objects and canvas and paint look like one single entity, in his case to provoke bafflement, showing things which looked whole but were impossible. This is what McKenna now was doing with the full colouring of this interior view, presenting his own painting on display, the view itself, the table top and balcony, but to the opposite effect, all alike bound together, though disrupting logic, scale and perspective.

'The Yellow Window' is one of a few of his paintings, all of this time, centred on a personable figure, though anonymous. She stares directly outside, while the artist inside the room looks over his books (perhaps about Claude and Poussin) and sees his painting, the view, and this person looking diminished beyond the greatly enlarged window opening. The painting is remarkably blonde, as the title says. This huge window separating inside and outside, the placing of the enigmatic woman in black, and the sheer weight of the saturated colour are all a tribute to the paintings of Edward Hopper. Hopper had an extraordinary skill to place flat, layered colour at a perfect tone to slot together with other shapes to make space, often to link inside and outside and, in addition, in his case, to create a warm erotic atmosphere. There is also a heavy sense of air in this painting by McKenna. But the mood is directed towards a positive re-creation of the past: the paintings of Claude and Poussin in Rome, the pagan and early Christian temples leaning together, and the church buildings and modern city now. The painting at the left has clearer colour than the 'real' view, as art is imposing, but best of all here are the interlocking angles of coloured pieces that lie on the surface, as in an abstract painting.

The same figure appears in the painting 'Plans and Ashes', the drawing for which (not with specific figures) is in this exhibition (p.108), and she is again mysterious in these paired scenes of double Annunciations, maybe of a beginning and an ending. The 'plan' is fragments of an ancient map of Rome, the 'ashes' an Etruscan urn from a burial chamber. Some of these chambers below the fields north of Rome have been arranged for visits, with steps downward underground and a light on a switch. To stand inside these empty tombs, absent of all sculpture, is to look at the mural paintings in earth colours that were meant to be seen only by the resurrected dead of two thousand years ago. They depict an assembly of the good things of the world, like a private collection, or a toy-cupboard. Since there is no Etruscan writing the intruder sees this accumulation of pleasurable scenes and architectural fragments without any literal understanding, but feeling a call from the past of a common culture and humanity. In McKenna's Italian paintings, such fragments are assembled, and similarly there is no narrative meaning except for sharing this past, and his constant linkage of areas of different status, as if a style of 'abstract thresholdism'.

There is a feeling within these paintings that someone has made a mental journey, and these are the places they have visited, where they had their dealings with various friends before departing, so that what we can now see is the trace of the differing emotional levels that make a life. The life may be fragmentary, but is made whole. The medium that expresses the moods and businesses of this life is that of colour. If one of these pictures were a piece of music, like the Mozart and Beethoven recordings in McKenna's studio now, then it would have a theme that recurs, in different keys or pitch or instrumentation, and then ends, but what is felt as most moving is the longing to grasp the ways that it changes every time, and slips from one effect to something else, so that it is the bearing between one change and another that carries an evolution.

The journey in 'Stone Map' is from an illustrated book, perhaps about Rome, and a box and a block of some kind, all lying along the foreground, to a similar block already painted in the painting, then to the stone map of Rome, a real object that has survived only as fragments (these were copied from a print by Piranesi in his Taschen book), and finally into a view from his balcony of the Aventine hill, one of the places in the map. The stretch and compromise of putting these things convincingly together forces a freer role onto colour, which here finds its strength in the odd yellows, reds and blacks of the sunlit buildings near the centre. This horizontal band of colour is not merely beautiful but also rather uncomfortable, seen below a row of unexplained black towers.

INTERIORS

McKenna's architectural paintings from about 1990, of interiors and of particular buildings, carry forward this feeling of revealing a visual journey between mental representations. Even the domestic 'Interior Galicia' (p.73), noticed when sitting at a table and looking into the next room in a friend's house, became for McKenna a painting of a complex route. The eye departs from a nice teacup off into a space with blocks and spheres of pure colour, zig-zagged along diagonals from tiles and carpet, towards the presence of some light that fills the invisible half of the other room.

He has often painted his Italian studios, either full of his new paintings around the walls or with a view into the garden outside, and the Tate's 'Large Studio at Castiglion' (p.78) is one of the largest of these pictures. It is devised so that the artist is looking at the spot where he would be standing to paint a still life, to be arranged on the trestle table. There is a sudden confusion of scale, with still lifes, houses and interiors looking much the same in the warm light. A basket as a metaphorical self is at the left, and opposite is a blue fabric placed as a stand-in for a model. Colours and objects are transformed into paintings, and even the far wall, with its five small pictures of open doorways, is given a false edge, as if it were itself some enormous painting. The room has the grandeur of the chancel of a church, where what is celebrated is the Italian light, revealed in the controlled tonality of yellow and orange. It is possible to watch the colours of the room and the paintings becoming light as the shadow falls across them, all looking the more strange as the artist's materials and clutter have been tidied up, or ignored. This is a triumph of painting light in a volume of space.

DOCK CITIES

At some point this sense in his paintings of a journey loosened its pervading sense of finitude, as McKenna toured for a period of years deliberately to study points of departure, looking at lighthouses, port cities and buildings, all places which mark the end of the near world. The array of his paintings of these places in this exhibition is astonishing, both for the way that these complex views are summarised, constructed sometimes from a mass of small areas of colour and sometimes from the opposite, a few simple forms. On a more prolonged encounter the pictures come to look abstract.

In Cedeira, a fishing town near Corunna in northern Spain, on a corner of Europe, McKenna seems to have deliberately chosen a building which with its glass-framed verandas on two sides, looking like some endless paint box, required the greatest number possible of small coloured areas to make its shape (p.71). It lies beside the port, and so shows watery reflections in the glass, as if the building itself were looking out to sea, and only anchored down by some drain pipes from a building site that happened to be in the foreground beside it. A close up watercolour of 'Lighthouse County Down' (p.129) appears as pristine as a Bauhaus painted construction. Another 'St John's Point' (p.100) lighthouse is also simple, but is especially like a painting by Hopper, except for its peculiar fortress walls and entrance, and its austere concentration, looking like some prison for exiles, with an unsettling route through and beyond.

The places that McKenna has visited to paint, even just those seen in paintings in this exhibition, reveal his compulsion towards the periphery: Porto, Dublin, Istanbul, Cedeira, Lisbon, Madeira, San Sebastian, Naples and Maladroxia (an island on the end of a causeway in the furthest corner of Sardinia). This is the case of a European artist at pains to examine the southern and western margins. Drawings and watercolours made in these places, seen from the street or from hotel balconies, were used to make large paintings in the studio in Ireland. 'Naples Harbour' (p.45) appears deserted, as if the traffic and people moved too quickly to be recorded, or perhaps that they had fled, along with all the business of the street. Vesuvius in the background is a reminder of McKenna's much earlier drawing and painting of Clio, in that what we are now looking at must be her 'Fifth Style', where the framing might have become the passing between the different degree of detail of fore- and middle- and back-grounds. But more likely it is that the degree of abstraction has so increased that the citizens simply do not feature. A cruise liner nuzzles into the buildings at the limit of the foreground. It is not quite possible to tell whether some parts of buildings are in the city or the ship, which is placed exactly parallel to the frame, and a visitor within the painting might be on dry land or might already be on board and unable to disembark. McKenna's ports are places of departure as much as are the paintings by Claude, but there is no sense of Claude's benevolent sunset eternity, and they as much resemble Mondrian's last abstract paintings of London and New York, with their beads of colour and optimistic but uncertain message.

The paintings of quayside buildings are the same in essentials as are the dock cities. A modernist dockside 'Custom House Lisbon' (p.68) occupies the middle of a painting, but it is balanced by an extraordinary foreground of abstract colour in perspective. This (no more than interesting) building is suddenly loaded with an effect of light and colour, popping into space as part of some quite different pictorial event contained within the colouring. And similarly the 'Alcantara Warehouse' (p.69) in the docks at Lisbon shows a full-on triptych of abstract paintings, in that odd area with high bridges over the Tagus where this building is sat down and taken from context. The purity and utility of marine structures have often appealed to modernist painters, and here the formal and real-world are re-united, Claude and Mondrian together, in a vision that confronts the entire arsenal of art against the opaque officialdom of exit.

Dock cities on a map are only half circles, the other half being the open sea, like complex structures that have been split in two and are missing their reflections. They are shown in full light, at dawn and dusk, and at night. Their rainbow colours come from the seaward side. What can it mean, this amazing accumulation of large paintings of these places, which are like nothing else? In his later painting of a different temple at Selinunte (p.39), McKenna saw the building not as solid, but as a screen for the open sea, like an entrance gateway. Whatever personal relevance they might have, these paintings also show as commensurable the frontier cities of Europe, from Istanbul around the edges to Dublin, all alike, in their different ways, at a moment when all can hold together.

The mural paintings by Ambrogio Lorenzetti in the city hall of Siena, for a long time admired by McKenna, are a precedent for this group. These show a huge unfolding of the (then) modern city, expressing its laws and markets and pleasures, and disasters, in a pair to contrast the effects of good and bad governance. There is an interlocking of observation and moralising, with individual detail dictating how the murals are organised, yet there for its purpose. They are overrun with people and trades, but are alike McKenna's cities in both means and intention. The mythic Siena appears as a network of coloured walls, windows, arcades and roofs, not as a local view, since its function was a moral example. Everyone would have known it was an ideal and not a real place. McKenna's patchwork cities also could not be mistaken for a study of geography, and this provokes a reflection on the nature of these points of escape.

Lorenzetti showed both town and country feeding from each other, and alongside these paintings of the future McKenna has continued to paint the riverbanks of the Barrow. This exceptionally attractive river is more or less beside his home, with tow-paths that extend both ways further than can be walked. These deceptive paintings are a response to sight of this river, as also a tribute to Constable and an exercise in avoiding the Pastoral in a pastoral place. They have a strange magnificence of colour, often scattering greenish leaves like pieces of a jigsaw that do not match but cannot be overlapped, in defence against further penetration. Some are a bit like the paintings of Harold Cohen, his Slade School tutor more than forty years earlier, as if the sight of nature has caught up with his own origins in English sixties abstraction. McKenna's eyes are trained, through studying still life, to see the gaps between things, and these foliage paintings are often screens of one row of bushes hiding another of trees (p.92), or bare branches intruding in front of the flooded river (p.95). The river in flood is a distant part of the delta of Poussin's 'Winter'.

THE PURSUIT OF PAINTING

As McKenna became through his career more expert in the practice of painting, he was able to simplify and concentrate the overt content of the pictures – "The fruit of decades of work and self-criticism is the discarding of what is irrelevant to it, opening the possibility of an even greater concentration on the essentials" (1997, p.20). This is from his essay that introduces 'The Pursuit of Painting', a group exhibition in Dublin he was invited by Declan McGonagle to curate for the Irish Museum of Modern Art in 1997, where he took the opportunity to assemble paintings by his 'cultural mentors' back to Bonnard, de Chirico and Derain, and by some admired contemporaries. The painters, including watercolour painters, that he selected were all able to achieve what might be called 'body' in their materials, a sense of heaviness and a glow of light – light that could be either light or dark – in the stuff their pictures are made of. Gwen John, Balthus, Scully and the others are alike in this, with little distinction between naturalism and abstraction, since it is the loading of the paint that comes first, and that counts, though the way in which the paint is used has to relate to the overt content, whether this is a seated model or a conjunction of parallels. The later paintings of Gwen John might speak of fortitude, self sufficiency, the settling of a character within and apart from the world, but the means are her successive visual commitments, adding to what was there already. Each touch contains a memory, and the subjects of all these paintings are the ways in which the artist takes possession of their look.

McKenna had sometimes worked in the studio of his friend the Munich artist Peter Schermuly, a colleague in the research into painting. After Schermuly had died his wife allowed McKenna to go back to the studio, which was still set up the way it had been, to paint a memorial (p.72). In the painting at the Tate of his own studio (p.78), everything looks inwards at what the artist sees, but this is now reversed. Schermuly's cast of the 'Dancing Faun', and the life size and apparently wounded lay figure with its left arm echoing the faun's, both look outwards to an empty space, where the illumination is framed in black cloth. All is coloured light or coloured shade, with no half-tones except in the painting on the easel of apples and pears in a basket. This is a demonstration – from the last work left unfinished, to the materials of art, to classical art, and to the lively-looking fruit in the living painting.

The elements of art, the pure colours in the patchwork at the left, the perspective and the few brushes and paints, are illustrated in simple examples. It is the inevitable message seen in a studio, that this artist turned colours into art, and this is where it was done. But McKenna's painting takes a monumental view, in which the interior has become large scale architecture. The people in McKenna's San Sebastian at 'Paseo la Concha' (p.65) are generic, like toys or like an opera chorus, and anyway half hidden, as the degree of abstraction does not take on the particular. Similarly the character and gestures of the lay figure in Schermuly's studio, with one arm raised, are not explainable, but have to do with its pose and with its relation to the bronze faun from Pompeii, and their shadows. A simple memorial becomes a statement about the means of painting and its sources ancient and modern. The dancing lay figure of the Clio drawing, there the Pied Piper who led the whole new parade, has become a figure of judgment, of a kind that seems in its golden yellow in front of the blue screen to be benign.

David Fraser Jenkins
June 2014

References

1981 Extracts from a conversation between Barry Barker and Stephen McKenna in Brussels, February 1981, The Orchard Gallery, Londonderry and Arts Council Gallery, Belfast

1984 Stephen McKenna, 'On Landscape', Berlin

1986 Richard Morphet, 'An English Oak Tree', Tate website

1990 Extracts from a conversation between Stephen McKenna and Murdoch Salmon Rome 1989, Manuela Boscolo Gallery, Busto Arsizio

1996 The Orchard Gallery, Derry

1997 Stephen McKenna, Introduction, 'The Pursuit of Painting', Irish Museum of Modern Art, Dublin

The Elements of Architecture

LARGE DORIC PILLAR K1310 160 × 120 cm 2013 Cat 1

ORTHOGONAL K1308 160×120 cm 2013 Cat.2

SMALL DORIC PILLAR K1309 75 × 50 cm 2013 Cat.3

SMALL HOMAGE TO VITRUVIUS K1307 50 × 65 cm 2013 Cat.4

PANTHEON K1316 100 × 80 cm 2013 Cat.5

SELINUNTE TEMPLE E K0205 100 × 150 cm 2002 Cat.6

SELINUNTE K8305 150 × 250 cm 1983 Cat.7

STONE MAP K9114 80 × 100 cm 1991 Cat.8

Cities and Ports

THE BAY OF NAPLES K0622 120 × 180 cm 2006 Cat.9

NAPLES HARBOUR K0719 150 × 200 cm 2007 Cat.10

SMALL NAPLES DAWN K0722 50 × 75 cm 2007 Cat.11

PORTO K0711 200 × 150 cm 2007 Cat.12

MARMARA EVENING K0813 90 × 120 cm 2008 Cat.13

MARMARA DAWN K0901 100 × 150 cm 2009 Cat.14

MADEIRA K0802 160 × 240 cm 2008 Cat.15

GREENWICH PARK K8406 200 × 250 cm 1984 Cat.16

CATHEDRAL AND PALACE PORTO K0717 90 × 120 cm 2007 Cat.17

PORTO BRIDGE AT NIGHT K0710 120 × 180 cm 2007 Cat.18

ISTANBUL DREDGER AT NIGHT K0814 60 × 90 cm 2008 Cat.19

LONDON CITY HALL K1403 50 × 40 cm 2014 Cat.20

BERLIN HAVELSEE K8405 200 × 300 cm 1984 Cat. 21

THE ITALIAN CONSULATE IN BERLIN K8413 200 × 275 cm 1984 Cat.22

THE CITY OF DERRY – THE FOYLE K8217/A 120 × 180 cm 1982 triptych left Cat.23

THE CITY OF DERRY – THE ARMS K8217/C 160 × 120 cm 1982 tryptich centre Cat.24

THE CITY OF DERRY – THE BOGSIDE K8217/B 120 × 180 cm 1982 tryptich right Cat.25 61

LIFFEY MORNING K1008 100 × 135 cm 2010 Cat.26

TARA STREET FROM LIBERTY HALL K1006 160 × 240 cm 2010 Cat.27

SAN SEBASTIAN K0907 120 × 160 cm 2009 Cat.28

PASEO LA CONCHA K1002 120 × 180 cm 2010 Cat.29

Buildings and Interiors

CUSTOM HOUSE LISBON K0819 120×180 cm 2008 Cat.30

CLAUSEWITZ BARBADOS K1113 120 × 160 cm 2011 Cat.32

CEDEIRA Ko920 135 × 100 cm 2009 Cat.33

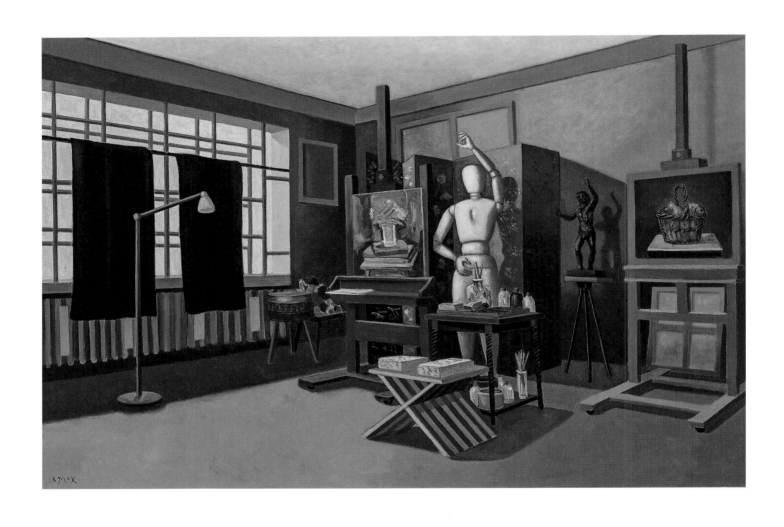

PETER SCHERMULY'S STUDIO IN MUNICH K0906 100 × 150 cm 2009 Cat.34

INTERIOR GALICIA K0918 120 × 90 cm 2009 Cat.35

HOMAGE TO PIRANESI K9006 80 × 100 cm 1990 Cat.36

THE YELLOW WINDOW K9007 120 × 160 cm 1990 Cat.37

WINDOW WITH CALABRIAN VASE K9705 150 × 120 cm 1997 Cat.38

ROMAN STUDIO K9002 100 × 150 cm 1990 Cat.39

LARGE STUDIO AT CASTIGLION K9365 120 × 160 cm 1993 Cat.40

PALOMBARO K8830 135×100 cm 1988 Cat.41

INTERIOR WITH FRESCOES K9216 50 × 70 cm 1992 Cat.42

Trees, Rivers and the Sea

PARAVENT K8402 four part screen each 182 × 62 cm 1984 Cat.43

AN ENGLISH OAK TREE K8111 200 × 150 cm 1981 Cat.44

NIGHT TREE K9923 100 × 80 cm 1999 Cat.45

TILLEA VULGARIS K0126 180 × 120 cm 2001 Cat.46

FOLIAGE K8345 20 × 30 cm 1983 Cat.47
OAK BRANCHES K8332 25 × 40 cm 1983 Cat.48

STUDY FOR RICHMOND PARK K8344 30 × 40 cm 1983 Cat.49
OAKS AND CHESTNUTS K8367 30 × 50 cm 1983 Cat.50

RAINY TREE K1407 60 × 50 cm 2014 Cat.51

FIG LEAVES K1213 80 × 100 cm 2012 Cat.52

HORSE CHESTNUT LEAVES K1212 120 × 90 cm 2012 Cat.53

BARROW TOWPATH K1210 100 × 150 cm 2012 Cat.54
BARROW TREES K1211 120 × 160 cm 2012 Cat.55

BARROW TREES WITH FIELD K0317 150 × 200 cm Cat.56

BARROW WEIR K0140 60 × 80 cm 2001 Cat.57

THE BARROW IN FLOOD K0924 120 × 160 cm 2009 Cat.58

THE IRISH COAST K8112 120 × 125 cm 1981 Cat.59

STILL LIFE OF THE SEA   K8010   70 × 100 cm   1980   Cat.60

PALMS AND LEAVES K1301 135 × 100 cm 2013 Cat.61

LIGHTHOUSE AT CASCAIS K0817 90 × 90 cm 2008 Cat.62

ST. JOHN'S POINT K9361 100 × 150 cm 1993 Cat.63

LIGHTHOUSE WITH SUN K9821 30 × 40 cm 1998 Cat.64

MOONLIGHT AND SEA K0014 50 × 60 cm 2000 Cat.65

MOONLIGHT WITH CLOUDS K0019 60 × 50 cm 2000 Cat.66

THE MILKY WAY K0221 80 × 60 cm 2002 Cat.67

Drawings and Watercolours

809

MALAGA TOWERS 0526/D 29 × 39 cm 2005 pencil Cat.68

GOODMAN'S YARD 1310/D 27 × 36 cm 2013 pencil Cat.69

STUDY FOR 'PLANS AND ASHES' 9102/W 30 × 42 cm 1991 watercolour Cat.70

STUDIO WITH FIGURE 0102/W 30 × 40 cm 2001 watercolour Cat.71

GARDEN HOUSE PESTANA 0604/D 39 × 57 cm 2006 pencil Cat.72

MARITIME MUSEUM GREENWICH 8418/D 28 × 38 cm 1984 pencil Cat.73

SANTA ANA LAS PALMAS 1030/D 29×38cm 2010 pencil Cat.74

SAN NICOLA IN CARCERE 9048/D 37 × 52 cm 1990 pencil Cat.75

PALATINO 8914/W 28 × 34 cm 1989 watercolour Cat.76

BERLIN BODE MUSEUM 1005/W 28 × 36 cm 2010 watercolour Cat.77

CATHEDRAL AND PALACE PORTO 0719/D 24 × 33 cm 2007 pencil Cat.78

THE BISHOP'S PALACE PORTO 0703/W 24 × 32 cm 2007 watercolour Cat.79

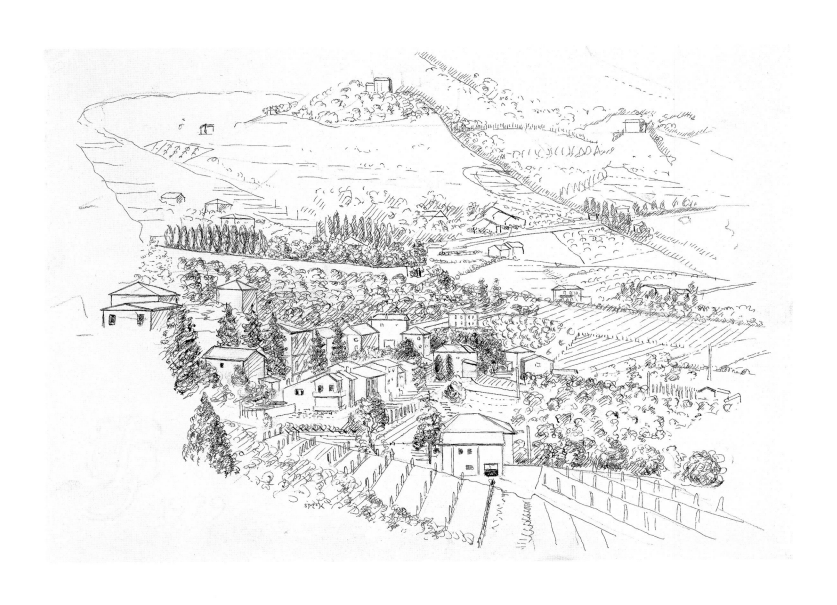

CASTIGLION FIORENTINO 9130/D 29 × 40 cm 1991 pen and ink Cat.80

SYCAMORE LEAVES 8413/D 34×51cm 1984 charcoal Cat.81

THE BOGSIDE DERRY 8113/W 28 × 39 cm 1981 pen and watercolour Cat.82

PITIGLIANO BIRDS 0513/D 39 × 57 cm 2005 pencil Cat.84

BIRDS AND TREES 0607/W 26 × 36 cm 2006 watercolour Cat.85

SKY WITH TWO BIRDS 8510/P 29 × 38 cm 1985 pastel Cat.86

SKYLINE 8414/D 28 × 38 cm 1984 red chalk Cat.87

FIVE SMALL ROCKS 9509/W 21 × 33 cm 1995 watercolour Cat.88
WAVE STRUCTURE 9503/W 19 × 28 cm 1995 watercolour Cat.89

DONEGAL SEA 8175/D 29 × 39 cm 1981 pencil Cat.90

27 v 19.   8 v v 6 v

LIGHTHOUSE COUNTY DOWN 9405/W 26 × 19 cm 1994 watercolour Cat.91

ROCK POOL 0407/D 36 × 50 cm 2004 charcoal Cat.92

STUDY OF TREES 8324/D 39×59 cm 1983 pencil Cat.93

STUDY FOR THE AGE OF REASON 8058/D 53×71 cm 1980 pencil Cat.94

CIRCE 8112/W 28 × 39 cm 1981 ink and watercolour Cat.95

STUDY FOR CLIO OBSERVING THE FIFTH STYLE 8525/D 51 × 70 cm 1985 pencil Cat.96

ODYSSEUS AND SIRENS 8114/W 35 × 25 cm 1981 pen and watercolour Cat.97

THE WARRIORS 8004/W 26 × 27 cm 1980 watercolour Cat.98

THE COMMANDER 8030/D 26 × 37 cm 1980 pen and ink Cat.99

RECEPTACLES 9602/W 32 × 48cm 1996 watercolour Cat.100

COLUMN 8925/W 57 × 38cm 1989 watercolour Cat.101

ETRUSCAN STONE 8309/W 25 × 17cm 1983 watercolour Cat.102

STONE WITH THREE HOLES 9704/W 26 × 36 cm 1997 watercolour Cat.103

26.4.'22

STILL LIFE 0523/D 29 × 23 cm 2005 pencil Cat.104

CALABRIAN VASES 9523/W 28 × 43 cm 1995 watercolour Cat.105

THE DEATH OF ROSSINI 8207/W 21 × 30 cm 1982 watercolour Cat.106

LOTHAR SCHMIDT MUELISCH 0220/D 39 × 26 cm 2002 pencil Cat.107

146   STEPHEN HARRAP 9233/D 21 × 26 cm 1992 charcoal Cat.108

BEN KIELY 0039/D 30 × 25 cm 2000 charcoal Cat.109

TIGER 1204/D 28×39 cm 2012 pencil Cat.110

TWO SNAKES 1201/D 29 × 38 cm 2012 pencil Cat.III

SMALL GORILLA 1207/D 32 × 25 cm 2012 pencil Cat.112

SWINE'S HEAD 8237/D 29 × 52 cm 1982 red and black chalk Cat.113

BARBADOS BIRDS 1109/D 39 × 56 cm 2011 pencil Cat.114

FIVE BIRDS 1206/D 39×28cm 2012 pencil Cat.115

NUDE 8289/W 29 × 40 cm 1982 watercolour and crayon Cat.116

FOUR LADIES IN NORFOLK 1311/W 19 × 29 cm 2013 watercolour Cat.117

Catalogue of works

PAINTINGS

Unless otherwise stated, works are from private collections in Ireland.
All paintings are oil on canvas.

1. LARGE DORIC PILLAR K1310 160×120 cm 2013 page 34 (Hugh Lane only)

2. ORTHOGONAL K1308 160×120 cm 2013 page 35 (Hugh Lane only)

3. SMALL DORIC PILLAR K1309 75×50 cm 2013 page 36 (Hugh Lane only)

4. SMALL HOMAGE TO VITRUVIUS K1307 50×65 cm 2013 page 37 (Hugh Lane only)

5. PANTHEON K1316×100×80 cm 2013 page 38

6. SELINUNTE TEMPLE E K0205 100×150 cm 2002 page 39 (mima only)
   Collection Irish Museum of Modern Art, Donation, IBRC, 2011

7. SELINUNTE K8305 150×250 cm 1983 page 40 (mima only)

8. STONE MAP K9114 80×100 cm 1991 page 41 (mima only)

9. THE BAY OF NAPLES K0622 120×180 cm 2006 page 44

10. NAPLES HARBOUR K0719 150×200 cm 2007 page 45 (mima only)

11. SMALL NAPLES DAWN K0722 50×75 cm 2007 page 46 (Hugh Lane only)

12. PORTO K0711 200×150 cm 2007 page 47 (mima only)

13. MARMARA EVENING K0813 90×120 cm 2008 page 48 (Hugh Lane only)

14. MARMARA DAWN K0901 100×150 cm 2009 page 49 (mima only)

15. MADEIRA K0802 160×240 cm 2008 page 50

16. GREENWICH PARK K8406 200×250 cm 1984 page 51

17. CATHEDRAL AND PALACE PORTO K0717 90×120 cm 2007 page 52 (mima only)

18. PORTO BRIDGE AT NIGHT K0710 120×180 cm 2007 page 53

19. ISTANBUL DREDGER AT NIGHT K0814 60×90 cm 2008 page 54 (Hugh Lane only)

20. LONDON CITY HALL K1403 50×40 cm 2014 page 55 (mima only)

21. BERLIN HAVELSEE K8405 200×300 cm 1984 page 56 (mima only)

DRAWINGS AND WATERCOLOURS

Exhibited only at mima

68. MALAGA TOWERS 0526/D 29 × 39 cm 2005 pencil page 106

69. GOODMAN'S YARD 1310/D 27 × 36 cm 2013 pencil page 107

70. STUDY FOR 'PLANS AND ASHES' 9102/W 30 × 42 cm 1991 watercolour page 108

71. STUDIO WITH FIGURE 0102/W 30 × 40 cm 2001 watercolour page 109

72. GARDEN HOUSE PESTANA 0604/D 39 × 57 cm 2006 pencil page 110

73. MARITIME MUSEUM GREENWICH 8418/D 28 × 38 cm 1984 pencil page 111

74. SANTA ANA LAS PALMAS 1030/D 29 × 38 cm 2010 pencil page 112

75. SAN NICOLA IN CARCERE 9048/W 37 × 52 cm 1990 pencil page 113

76. PALATINO 8914/W 28 × 34 cm 1989 watercolour page 114

77. BERLIN BODE MUSEUM 1005/W 28 × 36 cm 2010 watercolour page 115

78. CATHEDRAL AND PALACE PORTO 0719/D 24 × 33 cm 2007 pencil page 116

79. THE BISHOP'S PALACE PORTO 0703/W 24 × 32 cm 2007 watercolour page 117

80. CASTIGLION FIORENTINO 9130/D 29 × 40 cm 1991 pen and ink page 118

81. SYCAMORE LEAVES 8413/D 34 × 51 cm 1984 charcoal page 119

82. THE BOGSIDE DERRY 8113/W 28 × 39 cm 1981 pen and watercolour page 120

83. THE STONETHROWERS 0511/W 34 × 50 cm 2005 watercolour page 121

84. PITIGLIANO BIRDS 0513/D 39 × 57 cm 2005 pencil page 122

85. BIRDS AND TREES 0607/W 26 × 36 cm 2006 watercolour page 123

86. SKY WITH TWO BIRDS 8510/P 29 × 38 cm 1985 pastel page 124

87. SKYLINE 8414/D 28 × 38 cm 1984 red chalk page 125

88. FIVE SMALL ROCKS 9509/W 21 × 33 cm 1995 watercolour page 126   upper

89. WAVE STRUCTURE 9503/W 19 × 28 cm 1995 watercolour page 126   lower

90. DONEGAL SEA 8175/D 29 × 39 cm 1981 pencil page 127

91. LIGHTHOUSE COUNTY DOWN 9405/W 26 × 19 cm 1994 watercolour page 129

92. ROCK POOL 0407/D 36 × 50 cm 2004 charcoal page 130

Stephen McKenna

Born in London, 1939.
Lives in Carlow, Donegal and London

1959–64	Studied at the Slade School of Fine Art, University College, London
1965–67	Senior Lecturer in Painting, Canterbury College of Art
1971–73	Guest Artist, Bahnhof Rolandseck Germany
1984	Guest Artist, Deutsche Akademische Austauschdienst, Berlin
1995–96	Guest Professor, Hochschule für Bildende Künste, Braunschweig
1999	Member of Aosdána, Ireland
2001	Member of The Royal Hibernian Academy, Dublin
2005–09	President of the Royal Hibernian Academy, Dublin

ONE MAN EXHIBITIONS

2014	'Drawings and Watercolours 1974-2013', Butler Gallery, Kilkenny
2012	'The Paradise', The Douglas Hyde Gallery, Dublin
2010	Kerlin Gallery, Dublin
2007	Galeria Victor Saavedra, Barcelona
	'Contrasts and Complementaries', Kerlin Gallery, Dublin
2006	Galeria Estampa, Madrid
2005	The Royal Hibernian Academy, Dublin
	Galería Félix Gómez, Seville
2004	Kerlin Gallery, Dublin
	The Corridor Gallery, Reykjavik
	Fondación Antonio Pérez, Cuenca.
	The George Bernard Shaw Room, Carlow County Library.
2003	Douglas Hyde Gallery, Dublin

2002	Kerlin Gallery, Dublin
2000	Bahnhof Rolandseck, Remagen
	Kerlin Gallery, Dublin
1999	Cà di Frà, Milano
1998	Kerlin Gallery, Dublin
1997	Mestna Gallerija, Ljubljana
	Associazione d'Arte e Cultura Il Polittico, Roma
	Galerie Mönch, Bremen
1996	Orchard Gallery, Derry
	Reeds Wharf Gallery, London
1995	Kerlin Gallery, Dublin
	Reeds Wharf Gallery, London
1994	The Fruitmarket Gallery, Edinburgh
	Arts Council Gallery, Belfast
1993	Galerie Nikolaus Fischer, Frankfurt am Main
	Kerlin Gallery, Dublin
	Irish Museum of Modern Art, Dublin
1992	Kerlin Gallery, Dublin
	Galeria Estampa, Madrid
1991	Sala 1, Roma
	Casa Masaccio, San Giovanni Valdarno
1990	Manuela Boscolo Galleria, Busto Arsizio
	Galeria Estampa, Madrid
	Kerlin Gallery, Dublin
	Fenderesky Gallery, Belfast
	Galerie Inge Baecker, Köln
1988	Orchard Gallery, Derry
	Kerlin Gallery, Dublin
1986	Städtische Kunsthalle, Düsseldorf
	Edward Totah Gallery, London
	Galleria Seno, Milano

1985	Raab Galerie, Berlin
	Edward Totah Gallery, London
	Institute of Contemporary Arts, London
	Sander Gallery, New York
1984	Galerie Springer, Berlin
	Stedelijk van Abbe Museum, Eindhoven
1983	Galerie Micheline Szwajcer, Antwerpen
	Galerie Isy Brachot, Bruxelles
	Museum of Modern Art, Oxford
1982	Galerie Patrick Verelst, Antwerpen
1981	Orchard Gallery, Derry
	Arts Council Gallery, Belfast
1980	De Vereniging voor het Museum van Hedendaagse Kunst te Gent
	Sander Gallery, Washington D.C.
1979	Barry Barker Gallery, London
1978	Midland Group Gallery, Nottingham
	Barry Barker Gallery, London
	New 57 Gallery, Edinburgh
	Sander Gallery, Washimgton D.C.
1975	Galerie in Contra Club, Bonn
1974	Galerie Rutzmoser, München
1973	Städtische Sammlungen, Rheinhausen
	Galerie Röttger, Lünen
1971	Gallery Do Not Bend, London
1964	Galerie Olaf Hudtwalcker, Frankfurt am Main

JOINT EXHIBITIONS

2012	Stephen McKenna & Siobhan Hapaska, Kerlin Gallery, Dublin
2008	Stephen McKenna & Eithne Jordan, Fenton Gallery, Cork
2000	Stephen McKenna & Michael Williams, Art Trail, Cork
1998	'Light in Painting', Stephen McKenna & Chung Eun-Mo,
	Fenderesky Gallery, Belfast
1997	'Stones', Stephen McKenna & James Lee Byars, Douglas Hyde Gallery, Dublin

1992	McKenna/Picabia, Galerie des Beaux Arts, Bruxelles
1986	'Stephen McKenna und Peter Schermuly', Galerie Bismarckstrasse, Köln
1971	Stephen McKenna & Andrea Moering, Galerie Ostentor, Dortmund

GROUP EXHIBITIONS

2014	'Meditation on Plates', Casino Marino, Dublin
	'The Artist's Eye', Hunt Museum, Limerick
	'Things Go Dark', The Model, The Mall, Sligo
	'Keywords: Art, Culture and Society in 1980s Britain', Tate Liverpool
	'Paper i Cartró', Galeria Kewenig, Palma de Mallorca
	Annual Exhibition, The Royal Hibernian Academy, Dublin
2013	'Beasts of England, Beasts of Ireland', VISUAL Centre for Contemporary Art, Carlow
	'Still Life', Waterhouse & Dodd, London
	'Keywords', Iniva (Institute of International Visual Arts), London
	'Schau mich an! Porträts seit 1500', Arp Museum, Bahnof Rolandseck
	Annual Exhibition, The Royal Hibernian Academy, Dublin
2012	'Proper nouns and adjectives', Fenderesky Gallery, Belfast
	Members Exhibition, The Royal Hibernian Academy, Dublin
	'Time out of mind: works from the IMMA collection', Irish Museum of Modern Art, Dublin
	'Ever since I put your picture in a frame', Glasgow International Festival of Visual Art, 42 Carlton Place, Glasgow
	Kerlin Gallery, Dublin
	Annual Exhibition, The Royal Hibernian Academy, Dublin

2011 'The Surreal in Irish Art', Highlanes Gallery, Drogheda

'Interlude. (Aspects of Irish Landscape Painting)', The Douglas Hyde Gallery, Dublin

Annual Exhibition, The Royal Hibernian Academy, Dublin

2010 'The ING Discerning Eye Exhibition', Mall Galleries, London

'Changing Exhibition', Fenderesky Gallery, Belfast

'A Retrospective Exhibition 1979 – 2010' VISUAL Centre for Contemporary Art, Carlow

Annual Exhibition, The Royal Hibernian Academy, Dublin

2009 'To Have and Have Not', Kinsale Art Week, Cork

'Artist/Heaney/Books in Exhibition' Irish Museum of Modern Art, Dublin

'Invited Artists', Eigse Carlow Arts Festival

'In the extremest beyond concealment all bright stars', Fenderesky Gallery, Belfast

Annual Exhibition, The Royal Hibernian Academy, Dublin

2008 '"Make Straight for the Shore", An Exhibition of Irish Art', Strule Arts Centre, Omagh

'Fifty percent solitude', Kerlin Gallery, Dublin

'10,000 to 50. Contemporary Art from the Members of Business to Arts', The Irish Museum of Modern Art, Dublin

'Celebrating 20 Years. Gallery Artists', Kerlin Gallery, Dublin

'Exhibition of New Works', Fenderesky Gallery, Belfast

Annual Exhibition, The Royal Hibernian Academy, Dublin

2007 'Into Landscape' Macroom Town Hall Gallery. Travelling

'Turner Prize. A retrospective 1984 – 2000', Tate Britian, London

Annual Exhibition, The Royal Hibernian Academy, Dublin

2006 'Hearth. Concepts of Home' from the IMMA Collection in collaboration with Focus Ireland, Irish Museum of Modern Art, Dublin

Annual Exhibition, The Royal Hibernian Academy, Dublin

2005 'From Landscape', Mermaid Arts Centre, Bray. Limerick City Gallery

'The West as Metaphor', Royal Hibernian Academy, Dublin

'After the Thaw', Crawford Municipal Art Gallery

'Works on Paper', Fenderesky Gallery, Belfast

Annual Exhibition, The Royal Hibernian Academy, Dublin

2004 Annual Exhibition The Royal Hibernian Academy, Dublin

2003 'Triangolino', The Riverbank Arts Centre, Newbridge.

Annual Exhibition, The Royal Hibernian Academy, Dublin

2002 Konvention, Berlin

Annual Exhibition, The Royal Hibernian Academy, Dublin

2001 'Fenster & Interieurs', Galerie Inge Baecker, Köln

'Between Earth and Heaven", Museum voor Moderne Kunst, Oostende

2000 'An Artists' Century', The Royal Hibernian Academy, Dublin

'The Corridor – Twenty Years', Reykjavik

'AIB Art', Poznan, Poland

1999   'Inscriptions on Stones', Fenderesky
       Gallery, Belfast

       'La Pittura Ritrovata 1978–1998', Museo del
       Risorgimento, Roma

       'Oggetti Smarriti', Cà di Frà, Milano

       Annual Exhibition, The Royal Hibernian
       Academy of Arts, Dublin

1998   'Salon Vache', Galerie Art Store, Bruxelles

       'Academy without Walls', The Royal
       Hibernian Academy of Arts, Dublin

       'EV + A', Limerick

       'Vital Presence', Belltable Arts Centre,
       Limerick

1997   'Residue', Douglas Hyde Gallery, Dublin

       'Dreams & Traditions', Ulster Museum,
       Belfast and Smithsonian Institute,
       Washington D.C.

       Arte a Palazzo-Oraziana 1997, Licenza

1996   'Innovation from Tradition – Some Recent
       Irish Art', Bruxelles

1995   'Salut au Monde', Fries Museum,
       Leeuwarden, Bremen, Osnabruck

1994   'Hoffelijheden III', Centrum voor
       Kunsten, Begijnhof, Hasselt

1993   'Declarations of War', Kettle's Yard,
       Cambridge

1992   'Echec et Mat', Galerie des Beaux Arts,
       Bruxelles

       'Fin quando sara pittura', Galeria il
       Polittico, Roma

1991   'Paradise and other Parks', Arti et
       Amicitiae, Amsterdam

       'Riverberi della Malinconia', Galleria
       Manuela Boscolo, Busto Arsizio

       'Staatsporträt-Jubilaumsausstellung',
       Galerie Inge Baecker, Köln

       Opening Exhibition, Irish Museum of
       Modern Art, Dublin

       'Un alternativa Europea', Palazzo
       Bandera, Busto Arsizio, Palazzo dei
       Diamanti, Ferrara

1990   'Paysages', Galerie des Beaux Arts,
       Bruxelles

       'Il Mondo delle Torri da Babilonia a
       Manhattan', Palazzo Reale, Milano

1989   'A Vision of Ireland: 20th century Irish
       Painting', Herbert Art Gallery and
       Museum, Coventry

       'Art Sacré', Galerie des Beaux Arts,
       Bruxelles

       'Il Boscaiolo Magico e la Civetta', Galleria
       Pio Monti, Roma

       'The Advent Calendar', Gallery North,
       Kirkby Lonsdale

       'Blasphemies, Cries, Ectstasies',
       Serpentine Gallery, London

       'The Corridor – 5', Reykjavik

1988   'Pyramiden', Galerie Jule Kewenig, Berlin
       and Haus Bitz, Frechen

       'Europa', Kunstalle, Bremen

       '100 Years of Art in Britain', Leeds City
       Art Gallery

1987   'Avant Garde of the 80s', Los Angeles
       County Museum of Modern Art

       'Europe Eighty', Strasbourg, Dublin and
       tour

       'Reason & Emotion in Art', Edinburgh
       International

       'Selective View', Musées Royaux des Beaux
       Arts, Bruxelles

       'The Self-Portrait, A Modern View',
       Artsite, Bath and tour

       'The Blasted Oak', Herbert Art Gallery and
       Museum, Coventry

       'Memory and Imagination', Scottish Arts
       Council Touring Exhibition

1986   'Peter Moores No.8 Project: Out of Line',
       Walker Art Gallery, Liverpool

       'Falls the Shadow, Recent British and
       European Art', Hayward Gallery, London

       Turner Prize Exhibition, Tate Gallery,
       London

       'Current Affairs', Museum of Modern Art,
       Oxford

'Classical Spirit', San Francisco Museum of Modern Art

'Säulen/Columns', Galerie Jule Kewenig, Haus Bitz, Frechen

'Neo neo Classicism', Edith C Blum Art Institute, Bard College, New York

'Figure and Landscape', Edward Totah Gallery, London

1985 'Iterativismus', Galerie Bismarckstrasse, Köln

'The Irresistible Object: Still Life 1600-1985', Leeds City Art Galleries

'The Classic Tradition in Recent Painting & Sculpture', Richfield, Connecticut

'Wolfgang Amadeus Mozart', Neue Bilder, Galerie Ropac, Salzburg

'Idol', Raab Galerie, Berlin/Köln

1984 'The Hard Won Image', Tate Gallery, London

'Paravents', Schloss Loersfeld, Köln

'The British Art Show', Birmingham, Edinburgh, Southampton

'L'Art et le Temps', Palais des Beaux Arts, Bruxelles

1983 'New Art', Tate Gallery, London

'Collection A', Galerie Isy Brachot, Bruxelles

1982 'Documenta 7', Kassel

'Troie, Legende et Realité', Europalia Greece, Bruxelles

1980 'British Art 1940-80', Hayward Gallery, London

1979 'Europa 79', Kunst der 80er Jahre, Stuttgart

'Il Nuovo Contesto in Europa', Studio Marconi, Milano

1977 'Towards Another Picture', Midland Group Gallery, Nottingham

1972 'Intergroup 72', Städtische Sammlungen, Rheinhausen

1964 'Young Contemporaries', London

1963 'John Moores Liverpool Exhibition', Walker Art Gallery, Liverpool

WORKS IN PUBLIC AND CORPORATE COLLECTIONS

Irish Museum of Modern Art, Dublin
National Gallery of Ireland, Dublin
National Self Portrait Collection, Limerick
The Royal Hibernian Academy, Dublin
Ulster Museum, Belfast
Crawford Gallery, Cork
The Butler Gallery, Kilkenny
Allied Irish Bank Collection, Dublin
Bank of Ireland Collection, Dublin

The Arts Council of Great Britain
The British Council
Chelmsford and Essex Museum
The Government Collection
Imperial War Museum, London
Laing Art Gallery, Newcastle upon Tyne
Manchester City Art Gallery
Southampton City Art Gallery
Swindon Art Gallery
Tate Britain, London
University College London
Walker Art Gallery, Liverpool

Musées Royaux des Beaux-Arts, Brussels

Stiftung Stadtmuseum Berlin
Sammlung der Stadt Remagen
Städtische Sammlung Duisberg
Stiftung Hans Arp und Sophie Taeuber-Arp, Bahnhof Rolandseck

Fries Museum, Leeuuwarden, Netherlands

Fundación Antonio Pérez, Cuenca.

PUBLICATIONS

"Notes on Marat", *Art and Language*, Bd. 1, Nr. 2, Coventry 1969

"Notes to exhibition list", Gallery Do Not Bend, London, April 1971

"Caspar David Friedrich", *Studio International*, London 1972

"On Taste and Marine Pictures", *Sondern 3*, Zurich 1978

"Notes by the Artist", Catalogue *Stephen McKenna*, Midland Group, Nottingham 1978

"The Preparation for the Third Campaign", *Sondern 4*, Zurich 1979

"Parables of Painting – the Classical in the Past and Future", De Vereniging voor het Museum van Hedendaagse Kunst te Gent, 1980

"Pictor Classicus Sum; Giorgio de Chirico, Integrity and Reaction: *Artefactum*, Antwerpen, 1/1983

"On Landscape", Berliner Kunstlerprogramm des DAAD and Galerie Springer, Berlin, September 1984

Text in catalogue, *Second Sight*, Museum of Modern Art, San Francisco 1986

"Reply to a Curator", Brochure to *The Turner Prize*, Tate Gallery, London 1986

"Synopsis for a Drama", Catalogue *Edinburgh International*, Royal Scottish Academy, December 1987

"Notes on Walls", published under the title "The Forgotten Knowledge of Seeing", *Art and Design*, Bd. 4, Nr. 5/6, London 1988

"Reflections on a Dilemma", *Apollo Magazine*, London, July 1988

"Stones, Observations and Subjects", *Art and Design*, Bd. 4, Nr. 9/10, London 1988

"The Real Thing", Catalogue *Schermuly, Gegenstände*, Museum Wiesbaden, December 1989

"Confines and Qualifications", *Kunst und Museum Journaal*, Amsterdam Bd. 4, Nr. 4, 1993

"Extracts from a Sea Diary", *Art Review*, London, April 1995

Catalogue introduction *Feodora Hohenlohe-Oehringen*, 1995

Catalogue notes in *Stephen McKenna*, The Orchard Gallery, Derry 1996

Catalogue introduction *Nathalie du Pasquier*, Fenderesky Gallery, Belfast, Rubicon Gallery, Dublin 2000

Catalogue note "*Et in Arcadia Ego*", Douglas Hyde Gallery, Dublin 2003

Catalogue essay "*Academies*", Royal Hibernian Academy, Dublin 2003

"*The Barrow Book*", Carlow Local Authorities, Carlow 2004

"The Stereoscopic House", Catalogue *Eithne Jordan*, Ormeau Baths Gallery, Belfast 2004

"*The Royal Hibernian Academy School*" Royal Hibernian Academy Dublin 2005

Catalogue introduction *The Pursuit of Painting*, The Irish Museum of Modern Art, Dublin, Lund Humphries, London 1997

"Province and Metropolis", *Visual Artists' News Sheet*, issue 1 2005

Catalogue Essay "*The Royal Hibernian Academy School*", Royal Hibernian Academy, Dublin 2005

"Du Côté de Bran". Text by Maria Vela. Illustrations by Stephen McKenna. Galería Estampa, Madrid 2006

Pye's road to Damascus, *Irish Arts Review*, Spring 2013

"Observations and Reflections" Butler Gallery Kilkenny 2014

SELECTED BIBLIOGRAPHY

ALLTHORPE-GUYTON, MARJORIE
"Ministers of Misrule", Catalogue *The British Art Show* 1984

BARKER, BARRY
Interview in Catalogue Arts Council of Northern Ireland, Derry and Belfast 1981

BRIZZI, ARNALDO ROMANI
Catalogue Il Polittico Rome 1997
Catalogue *La Pittura Ritrovata 1978-1998* Museo del Risorgimento, Rome 1999

BUSTARD, JAMES
Catalogue Memory and Imagination Scottish Arts Council, 1988

BYARS, JAMES LEE
"Ten Extracts from a Conversation with James Lee Byars" Catalogue Irish Museum of Modern Art, Dublin 1993

CALVESI, MAURIZIO
Catalogue Sala 1 Rome, 1991

COHEN, DAVID
"Classicism and the Art of McKenna and Cox" *Artline* February 1989

COLLINS, DR. JUDITH
"Stephen McKenna – Recent Paintings" Catalogue The Orchard Gallery, Derry 1996

COMPTON, MICHAEL
Catalogue *New Art* Tate Gallery, London 1983
Catalogue *Viewpoint* Musées Royaux des Beaux-Arts, Brussels 1987

DALY, JANET
Catalogue Gallery Do Not Bend, London 1971

DELANY, GREGORY
Interview in *Rant*, Dublin May 1988

DUNNE, AIDÁN
Interview *Sunday Tribune* 19 September 1993
Interview *Irish Times* 2005

EBBINGE WUBBEN, J. C.
"Looking Back in Admiration as a Regenerating Force" Catalogue Institute of Contemporary Arts, London 1985

ELLIOTT, DAVID
"A Painter of Modern Life" Catalogue Museum of Modern Art Oxford, 1983

FALLON, BRIAN
Catalogue Kerlin Gallery, Dublin 1990
Interview *Irish Times* 26 August 1993

FEAVER, WILLIAM
"Allusions Veiled and Classical" *Art News* Bd. 85, January 1986.

FRIDJÓNSSON, HELGI PORGILS
Interview *Morgunbladid*, Reykjavik November 2003

FUCHS, RUDI
Catalogue Stedelijk van Abbe Museum Eindhoven, 1984

GONZÁLEZ, ÁNGEL GARCÍA
Catalogue Galeria Estampa, Madrid 1990
Catalogue *McKenna/Picabia* Galerie des Beaux Arts, Brussels, 1992
"'El Mundo es Muy Grande...' o El Pintor en Casa" Fundación Antonio Pérez, Cuenca 2004 and Royal Hibernian Academy 2005

HAMMACHER, A.M.
"L'Eternel Retour" Catalogue Galerie Isy Brachot, Brussels 1983

HARTEN, JÜRGEN
Introduction Catalogue Städtische Kunsthalle Düsseldorf, 1986

HUTCHINSON, JOHN
"Et in Arcadia Ego", Catalogue Douglas Hyde Gallery, Dublin 2003

JEFFREY, IAN
"In Touch with History: Paintings by Stephen McKenna" Catalogue Museum of Modern Art Oxford, 1983
"Current Comment" *Creative Camera* Nr. 241, January 1985
"McKenna and Clemente" *London Magazine*, 1986
"A Painter's Life" Catalogue Irish Museum of Modern Art, Dublin 1993

JENCKS, CHARLES
"Post Modernism" Academy Editions, London 1987

KELLY, DR. LIAM
Foreword in Catalogue The Orchard Gallery, Derry 1996

LIEBMANN, LISA
"Misty Channels" *Art Forum*, October 1985

LOTTINI, OTELLO
Introduction Exhibition Catalogue *Arte a Palazzo-Oraziana*, Licenza 1997

LUCIE-SMITH, EDWARD
"The Self Portrait, A Modern View" Sarema Press, London 1987

MAC GIOLLA LÉITH, CAOIMHÍN
"Retrospectively Speaking", *Social and Personal*, September 1993

McAVERA, BRIAN
Interview. "Capturing the Fleeting Eternal", *Irish Arts Review*, Dublin Autumn 2005

McGONAGLE, DECLAN
Foreword to Catalogue Institute of Contemporary Arts, London 1985
Foreword to Catalogue Irish Museum of Modern Art, Dublin 1993

MIRFENDERESKY, JAMSHID
"Light in Painting" Catalogue *Chung Eun Mo / Stephen McKenna* Fenderesky Gallery, Belfast 1998

MORPHET, RICHARD
Catalogue *The Hard Won Image* Tate Gallery, London 1984
Entry in *The Tate Gallery Catalogue of Acquisitions 1982-1984*

MORRIS, LYNDA
"An English View of Stephen McKenna" *Artefactum*, Antwerpen 1983

MOSEBACH, MARTIN
"Stephen McKenna – ein Zeitgenosse durchbricht die römische Mauer" Catalogue Städtische Kunsthalle Düsseldorf, 1986

NEMECZEK, ALFRED
"Neue Klassizisten: Rückkehr zum Mythos" *Art* , Hamburg 1983

PETTITT, YVONNE
"Stephen McKenna: Traditional Painter", M.Phil thesis, Trinity College Dublin 2010

POSER, MICHAEL VON
"Prefatory Notes" Catalogue Institute of Contemporary Arts, London 1985

PYLE, HILARY
"Stephen McKenna – New Landscapes" Catalogue Kerlin Gallery, Dublin 2000

SALMON, MURDOCH
Interview in Catalogue Galleria Manuela Boscolo, Busto Arsizio 1990

SCHMIDT-MÜHLISCH, DR. LOTHAR
"Das Ende der Naivität", Catalogue Städtische Sammlungen Rheinhausen 1973
"Von Schiess-Stand zu Palette", *Bonner Rundschau* , Bonn 14 November 1973
"Schweinskopf, Gefroren", *Die Welt*, Bonn 3 November 1984
"Virtuelle Wege ins Paradies", Catalogue Bahnhof Rolandseck, Remagen 2000

SINDEREN, WIM VAN
Introduction "Paradise and Other Parks" *art I 8*, Amsterdam 1991

SYRING, MARIE-LUISE
"Über die Sichtbarkeit und: einige Bemerkungen über die Postmoderne zum Schluss" Catalogue Städtische Kunsthalle Düsseldorf, 1986

THOMPSON, JON
Intoduction to catalogue Midland Group Nottingham 1978
"The Warning Hand", Catalogue Raab Galerie Berlin 1985
"McKenna Before the Walls of Pompeii", *Wolkenkratzer* 1/1987
"Illuminants and Illuminations", Catalogue Bahnhof Rolandseck, Remagen 2000

VAN TIGHEM, JEAN-PIERRE
"Je ne suis pas un artiste, je suis un peintre" Catalogue *McKenna/Picabia* Galerie des Beaux Arts, Brussels 1992

TIPTON, GEMMA
"The art of learning", *The Irish Times Magazine*, 13 October 2007

VETTESE, ANGELA
"Europe and America: Two Aspects of the New Surreal" *Flash Art*, April 1985

WALKER, DOROTHY
"Modern Art in Ireland" The Lilliput Press, Dublin 1997

WALSH, SAMUEL
Interview, *Circa* Summer 1997

Colophon

This catalogue has been published on the occasion of the exhibition *Stephen McKenna, Perspectives of Europe 1980 – 2014* at Middlesbrough Institute of Modern Art from February 6th to June 7th 2015
and at Dublin City Gallery The Hugh Lane from July 22nd to October 4th 2015

Exhibition and catalogue concept: the artist

Catalogue preparation, typesetting, colour reproduction and printing:
Jan van der Most, Düsseldorf

Photography:

Reproductions – Gillian Buckley, John Kellett, Dennis Mortell, the artist

Selinunte 1983, p.2; *Braunschweig 1984*, p.156 – Maria Gilissen

The Artist's Studio 2007, p.162 – Dylan Vaughan

Published by:
Middlesbrough Institute of Modern Art
Dublin City Gallery The Hugh Lane

ISBN: 978 0 86083 101 3

Stephen McKenna is represented in Ireland by the Kerlin Gallery, Dublin.

Other galleries include Fenderesky Gallery, Belfast; Galerie Estampa, Madrid